THE AMAZING MATH JOURNEY

2

TIME AND DIRECTION

www.royalcollins.com

THE AMAZING MATH JOURNEY

2

TIME AND DIRECTION

Written and illustrated by

Youdao Joyread Editorial Board

RC

Books Beyond Boundaries

ROYAL COLLINS

The Amazing Math Journey
Volume 2: Time and Direction

Written and illustrated by Youdao Joyread Editorial Board
Editorial Board Members: Yan Jiarui, Cui Yao, and Wang Dandan
Illustrator: Yan Jiarui

First published in 2024 by Royal Collins Publishing Group Inc.
Groupe Publication Royal Collins Inc.
BKM Royalcollins Publishers Private Limited

Headquarters: 550-555 boul. René-Lévesque O Montréal (Québec) H2Z1B1 Canada
India office: 805 Hemkunt House, 8th Floor, Rajendra Place, New Delhi 110 008

ISBN: 978-1-4878-1171-6

To find out more about our publications, please visit www.royalcollins.com.

Character Profile

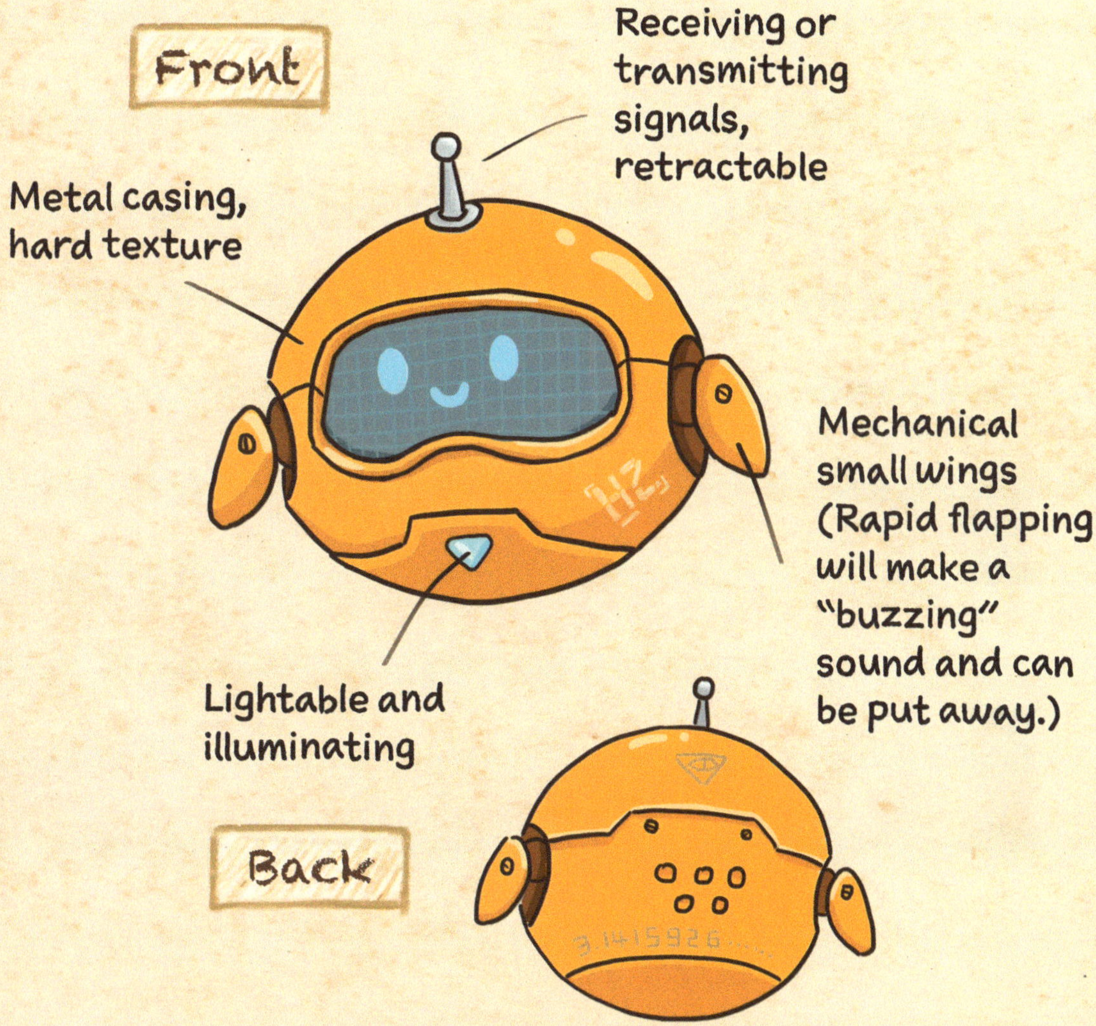

Yolk Pie

An intelligent machine ball with a wealth of knowledge whose weakness is being afraid of the dark is born somewhere on earth. The number is 3.1415926 . . . Because it is too long to remember, the Little Fox named it "Yolk Pie."

LOST?

Is the mystery partner seeking help?

SPACESHIP TIME MISALIGNMENT?

What kind of **ADVENTURE** will Little Fox experience next?

It's all documented here . . .

HURRY!

Open the diary and follow Little Fox to start the **ADVENTURE** together!

Contents

TIME AND DIRECTION

Chapter 1

Partners

Location: Math Planet   Weather: Clear

I was asleep at my desk when I heard a familiar yet unfamiliar voice in a **HALF-AWAKE** daze. I struggled to open my eyes and saw a round thing floating in mid-air, flashing an eerie **BLUE-GREEN** light . . .

"Ah!" I cried out in surprise, suddenly wide awake. I rubbed my eyes, doubting if I was dreaming, and pinched my arm hard.

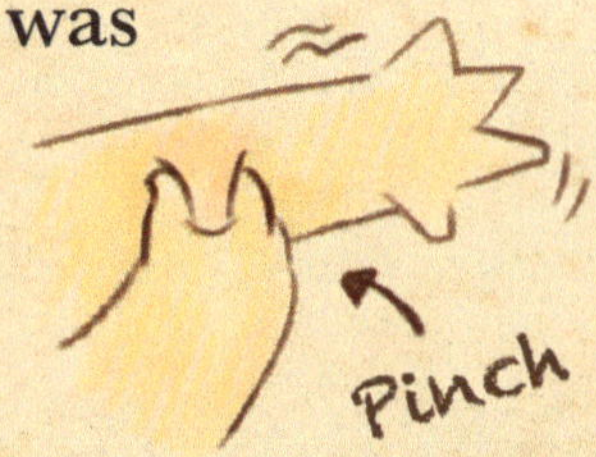

"Ouch! That hurts, hiss . . ."

I grimaced in pain, confirming that this was not a dream.

This machine ball, about the size of a soccer ball, was quickly flapping its little wings and moving up and down in front of me. It turned out that the flapping made the strange noise of its wings.

"Who . . . who . . . who . . . who are you? How did you come to my house?"

I was taken aback, and because I was so nervous, I stuttered a little as I stepped back cautiously.

The ball blinked its eyes on the display screen and suddenly spoke!

"I only remember being suddenly swept away by a black hole . . ."

"**BLACK HOLE**?" Did it also encounter a black hole like me?

Flight Menu

This flying ball is about the size of a soccer ball.
Buzzing
Buzzing
Who are you?
A talking ball?
How did you get to my house?

My sudden curiosity made me relax my guard, and I looked at it curiously.

This flying ball told me it came from earth, but for some reason, it suddenly encountered a black hole, was swept into another time and space, and lost many memories, unable to return. After seeing me, it had a special feeling toward me.

"Oh, you've been following me since we met?"

"Yep."

"What's your name then?"

"My identification number is 31415926 5358 9793 23846 . . ."

"Wait, wait, wait a minute . . ."

I interrupted. The number was too long. If I had to say everything every time I called it, it would be too troublesome!

"3—1—4—1—5—9—2—6 . . ."

I muttered to myself as I thought about it.

This identification number was quite special, similar to pi. I looked up at it; it was round, like a yellow ball, so I had a sudden idea.

"Then, I'll call you 'Yolk Pie'!"

"Good! Yolk Pie! I like this name!"

"Haha, I'm Little Fox. So, we're partners now!"

After meeting Yolk Pie, my new friend, I decided to help it return home! The thought of embarking on a new adventure made my pulse THROB WITH EXCITEMENT.

I packed up the equipment I needed on the way, then let Yolk Pie hide in my backpack for now, preparing to set off.

I didn't expect it to look small but takes up a lot of space, just barely fitting . . .

I slowly opened my bedroom door and carefully hid my BULGING school bag behind me.

"Mom, I'm going to help you take out the trash."

Taking out the trash was just an excuse. I grabbed the garbage bag and ran out before my

parents could react. I arrived in the basement and started up the spaceship.

"Okay, come out now."

Yolk Pie flapped its little wings and suddenly rushed out of the school bag, looking pitiful.

"Ah—I can finally come out—ah—I was suffocating—phew!"

It looked so funny that a mechanical ball had made itself look like it was about to suffocate.

"Hahaha! Yolk Pie, do you also need to breathe air?"

As soon as I finished speaking, I saw blushes on both sides of its display screen.

"I . . . I . . . it's because your school bag is too small!"

It was afraid of the dark but still tried to cover it up. However, seeing how shy it was, I didn't push it.

I set the destination of the spaceship as "Earth" and then pressed the time travel button. In the blink of an eye, we traveled to a piece of land.

A wave of heat hit me as soon as I opened the spaceship door.

"It's too hot here! Yolk Pie, is this your home?"

Knowledge Secret

$$\frac{\text{Circumference of button}}{\text{Diameter of button}} = 3.1415926 \ldots$$

Circular button

Whether it's a small circular **button** or a larger circular **plate** when you divide the circumference of a circle by its diameter, the answer will always be 3.1415926 … This number is infinite. We call it "**pi**," usually represented by the Greek letter π.

π is a key value used to calculate the area and circumference of circles and the volume of spheres.

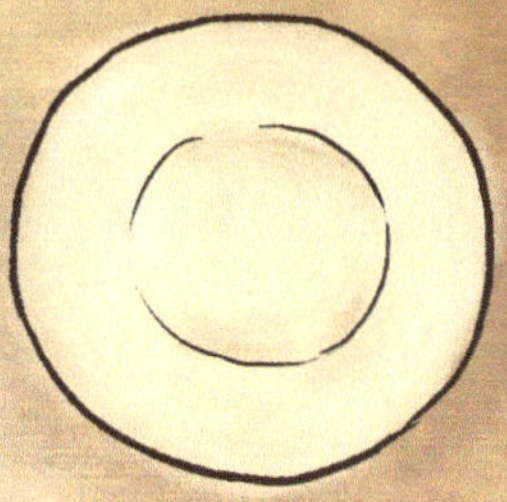

Circular plate

$$\frac{\text{Circumference of plate}}{\text{Diameter of plate}} = 3.1415926 \ldots$$

March 14 every year is known as "International Pi Day."

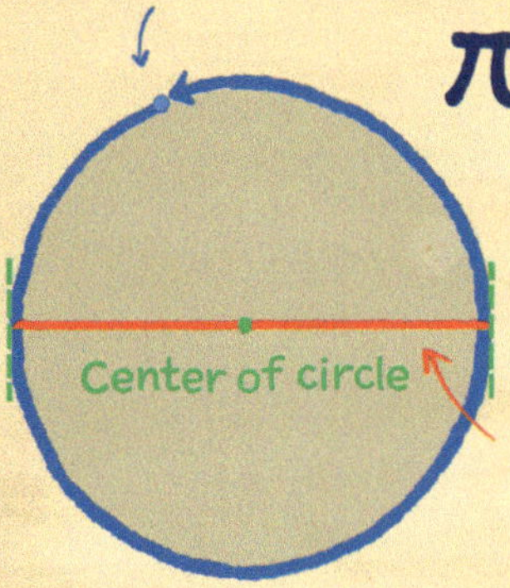

$$\pi = \frac{\text{Circumference}}{\text{Diameter}} = 3.1415 \ldots$$

π = Pie?

Yolk Pie's number is 31415926 5358 9793 23846 …

Chapter 2

The Golden Crow

Location: Earth Weather: Clear

The land here is cracked into many pieces, some big and some small. Only a few withered trees are around, without any signs of life. Suddenly, I looked up and saw something in the sky above me.

"There are ten suns!"

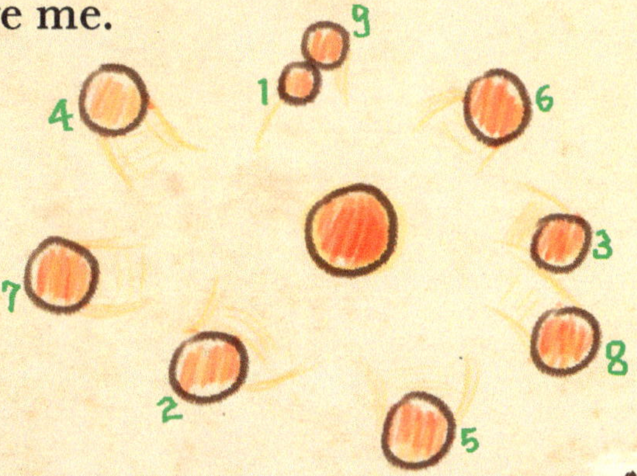

Yolk Pie shook his head. "No! There's only one sun on earth. This place . . . doesn't seem like home."

I looked up again and realized that nine of them were fireballs, shining brightly like the sun. This was bad news! These fireballs seemed to be flying toward the ground and getting CLOSER AND CLOSER to us!

"Yolk Pie, hurry! Let's go back to the spaceship!"

I quickly brought Yolk Pie back to the spaceship. We decided to time travel again to avoid being hit by the falling fireballs. But the spaceship sounded an alarm when I pressed the time travel button!

"ALERT! ALERT! The system temperature was too high. Time travel failed! Time travel failed!"

At that moment, a big fireball crashed not far ahead, turning the ground into black charcoal.

More fireballs began to fall, but luckily, the spaceship wasn't hit. However, the temperature around us became even hotter, and we were starting to feel suffocated.

"No, we must fix the spaceship system as soon as possible and get out of here!"

"How can we fix the system?" Yolk Pie asked anxiously.

"Well . . . we need to activate the cooling device, but we need enough water."

So Yolk Pie and I decided to find a water source.

We endured the heat and crossed one mountain after another. By now, my clothes were soaked with sweat, sticking tightly to my body, which made me very uncomfortable. We continued walking for a while and suddenly saw a huge black rock. Upon closer inspection, we found some mysterious patterns carved on the rock.

Yolk Pie flew to the front of the rock and stared at the patterns for a long time . . .

"I think . . . I've seen this pattern before . . ."

"This is the sun!" Yolk Pie said confidently.

"The sun? With a bird inside?"

I thought Yolk Pie must have been mistaken. How could there be a bird inside the sun? The temperature at the sun's center was so high that the bird would be burned to death.

But Yolk Pie nodded and continued, "This is **BIRD JINWU**, a golden crow with three legs. Legend has it that it flies from the east to the west every day, and the sun also rises in the east and sets in the west, thus forming the most basic unit of time on earth—a **DAY**."

"Wait, Yolk Pie, how did you know all this?" I looked at it curiously.

"I don't know either, but after seeing these patterns, I have regained some memories," it replied.

"Do you remember where your home is?" I asked it eagerly.

Yolk Pie thought for a moment and then shook its head. Although I was a bit disappointed, I still comforted it. I thought that it might need more

The temperature on the sun's surface is about 5,500°C, while the temperature at the sun's center is around 20,000,000°C.

information to recall its memories . . .

We walked around the rocks and continued forward, with more and more plants appearing around us. A gust of wind blew in our faces, mixed with the smell of **DAMP SOIL**! I knew that the water source must be nearby. I jogged a few steps and faintly heard the sound of water flowing, so I turned around and called Yolk Pie, then hurried forward.

"Haha, water! Yolk Pie, we found water!"

I took out the foldable water bottle from my backpack and filled all the water bottles to the brim. The breeze blowing on the water's surface was refreshing, and I unconsciously relaxed, leaning against a large rock, and fell asleep . . .

"Little Fox, wake up, wake up! It's already late morning! The sun has risen three poles high."

"THE SUN HAS RISEN THREE POLES HIGH? What do you mean?"

I rubbed my eyes sleepily and didn't understand what Yolk Pie was saying.

"It's not early anymore! Look, the sun has risen to three poles above the ground. The time should be between 9:00 a.m. and 11:00 a.m., according to the sun's height. We can roughly estimate the time based on the height of the sun."

"What? I slept for so long!"

I quickly got up, put the water-filled bottles into my backpack, and returned with Yolk Pie along the same path.

The water in the backpack was too heavy, so our return journey was slower. When we returned to the spacecraft, the sun had completely set, and the sky was dotted with stars.

I poured the water into the cooling system, and soon the spacecraft system returned to normal.

"Haha, the system is finally back to normal! Now what's next . . . hey hey hey hey . . ."

I hadn't finished speaking when I accidentally slipped and pressed the spacecraft's time-travel button!

Time travel—

Knowledge Secret

The sun is also called the "Golden Crow"

In ancient Chinese mythology, the sun that radiates golden light is said to be a black crow with three legs. That's why the sun is also called the "**GOLDEN CROW**."

Golden Crow = The sun ?

Xihe Gives Birth to Ten Suns

An ancient Chinese mythology

According to the *Classic of Mountains and Seas*, the goddess of the sun, **Xihe**, gave birth to ten children, the ten suns. In the East, there is a place called Tanggu, with a big tree named "Fusang." The ten suns lived on this big tree several thousand *zhang* tall (1 *zhang* ≈ 11 ft.). Only **1** sun goes on duty daily, and the other **9** rest on the tree.

The alternation of day and night provides the most basic unit of time for human beings—"day."

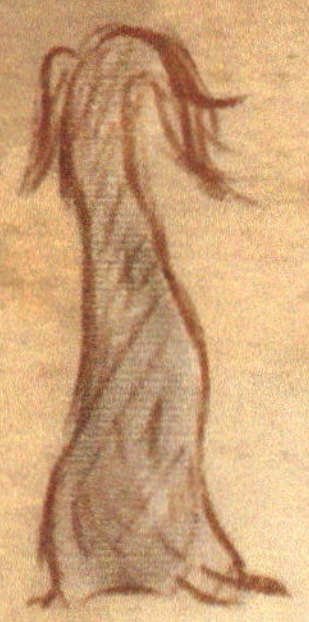

Every morning, the sun on duty rises from the Fusang tree in the east and transforms into the golden crow, flying from east to west. It lands on the Ruomu tree in the west in the evening. Day after day, the sun cycles, bringing light and warmth to people.

Bronze sacred tree

There are 9 birds on the tree, as 1 is on duty.

Q How much longer will the sun set in the picture below?

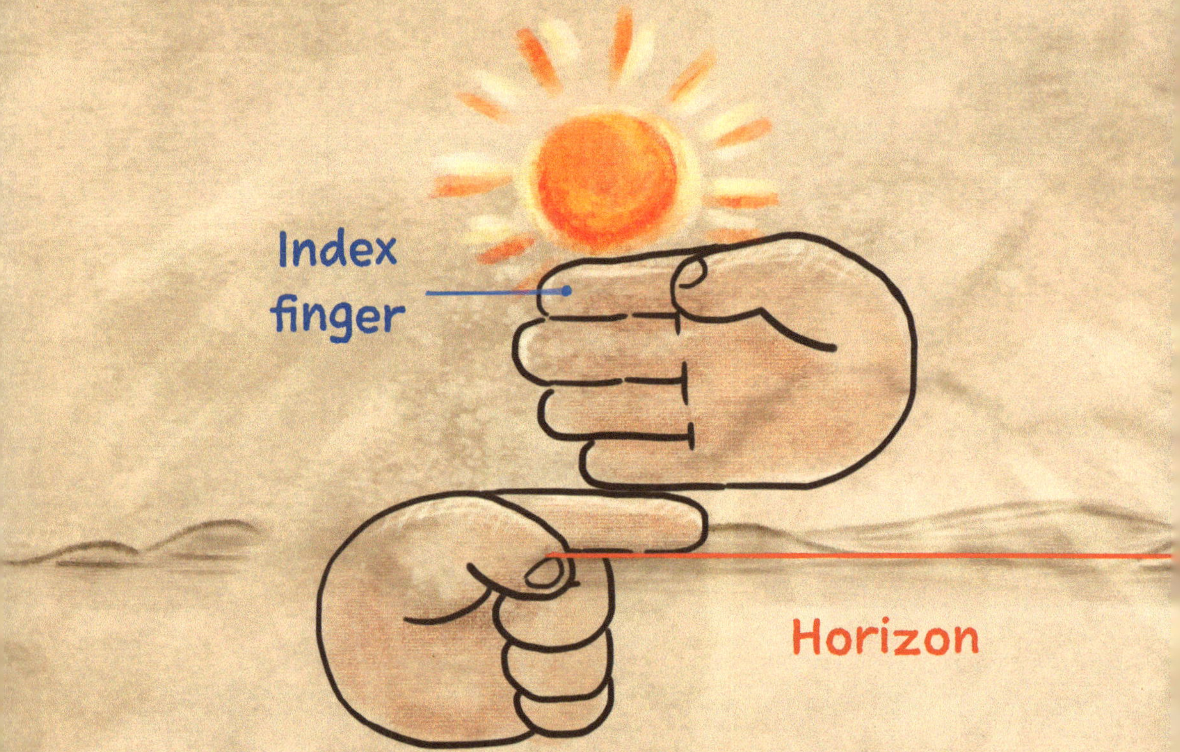

Ancient people could roughly estimate the time by the sun's height. Sometimes, we can also use this method to estimate the time. For example, when climbing a mountain without a watch or phone, do you know how to determine how much time is left before the sun sets?

Secret Incredibly, our hands are the only tool needed to estimate the time!

1. Face the sun and stretch your arm in front of you with your palm facing yourself.
2. Place your index finger directly beneath the sun, parallel to the horizon.
3. Count how many finger widths there are from the bottom of the sun to the horizon? (Each finger represents 15 minutes.)

The number of fingers × 15 mins. = The time until the sun sets

Chapter 3

The Day of the Full Moon

Location: Earth   Weather: Cloudy to fine

In the blink of an eye, our spaceship took us to another place. The moon was hidden behind thick clouds, emitting a faint light. With the help of the spaceship's lights, we could vaguely see that we were now on a small island in the middle of a lake.

Yolk Pie whispered in my ear, "Ah! It's so dark here. I don't like the night. When I was born, it was sunny. If it weren't for . . ."

"Hmm? Wait a minute, what did you just say?" I suddenly interrupted Yolk Pie, as if I heard some important information.

"Ah? I said I don't like the night," Yolk Pie whispered.

"No, not that sentence, the next one!" I became anxious.

"When I was born . . . it was sunny . . ."

Yolk Pie suddenly froze, and stopped in mid-air, as if he remembered something.

"Ah, I remember now! I was born at noon!"

"Uh-huh, and then what? And then what?" I asked eagerly.

"Then . . . then I don't remember . . ." Yolk Pie sighed.

"Ah!" I sighed deeply. Helping Yolk Pie get home wasn't as easy as I thought.

At that moment, a "**BANG**" came from the distant sky, and my attention was immediately drawn there.

"What was that sound?" I asked.

"It's fireworks, look!" Yolk Pie pointed in the direction of the sound.

I looked in the sound's direction and saw a beautiful red firework exploding in the distance like a gorgeous flower, but it disappeared in a moment.

"That was amazing! Let's get closer and look!" I said, still wanting more.

"But . . ." Yolk Pie hesitated.

"Maybe other fun things besides fireworks can help you remember! Let's go look!"

I said, walking in the direction of the fireworks.

"Wait . . . wait . . . wait for me!" Yolk Pie followed closely behind like a puppy.

We passed a long arched wooden bridge and came to the shore of the lake.

At that moment, fireworks exploded in the sky, making a DEAFENING SOUND and lighting the night sky. They looked like colorful flowers blooming in the sky.

"Wow, that's so cool!" I stared at the fireworks in the sky, lost in thought. It was beautiful.

"Look over there, Little Fox!"

Yolk Pie pointed in a different direction. I saw a giant lantern standing like a Ferris wheel in front of a city gate not far away, covered in countless lanterns, shining brightly. It was magnificently illuminated with brilliant fireworks.

"Wow, this is so spectacular!" I couldn't help but praise it.

The crowd on the streets of the city was bustling and lively. Everyone was dressed beautifully, strolling and admiring the lanterns that lined the streets. There were lotus lanterns, jade tower lanterns, green lion lanterns, embroidered ball lanterns, crab lanterns, white elephant lanterns . . . all kinds of lanterns, really DAZZLING!

Lanterns bright,
scattered in sight.
Gardens deep,
shining with light.
Like flowers fair,
so bright and rare.
Gates unlocked,
with paths to share.

喜庆元宵

Suddenly, I felt a pair of eyes staring at us from the dark, so I quickly turned my head and looked around, but I didn't see anyone strange. Instead, our outfits seemed a little out of place in the crowd.

To avoid drawing attention, I hid my Yolk Pie in my backpack and put my hat on my head.

"What festival is it today? Why is it so lively here?"

My Yolk Pie popped out of my backpack, using its little wings to point at the moon. By now, the clouds had cleared, and a round, bright moon hung in the night sky.

"It must be the 15th day of the lunar calendar today, and with so many people carrying lanterns, we must have stumbled upon the Lantern Festival here."

"What? The 15th day of the lunar calendar? The Lantern Festival? We don't have that holiday on our Math Planet." I was completely puzzled.

"The shape of the moon changes regularly, and when it becomes a **FULL MOON**, it's the **15TH DAY OF THE LUNAR CALENDAR**!"

I still didn't understand how my Yolk Pie figured that out.

At this moment, the crowd suddenly became agitated, and they all rushed to the sides of the street, leaving a middle path open.

I struggled to squeeze to the front of the crowd, only to see a carriage coming along the road, carrying something covered in cloth that looked a little strange.

People were talking about it, but I felt like I recognized it . . .

As the carriage passed me, I saw what was inside under the fluttering cloth. I was stunned and couldn't help but open my mouth wide—

"Ah!" I yelled, immediately covering my mouth and running out of the crowd.

"Yolk Pie, they seem to have . . . taken away my . . . spaceship!"

My mind went blank, and I became almost **INCOHERENT**.

By now, I couldn't hear the noisy crowd around me, and my mind was a mess . . .

Knowledge Secret

Moon Phases

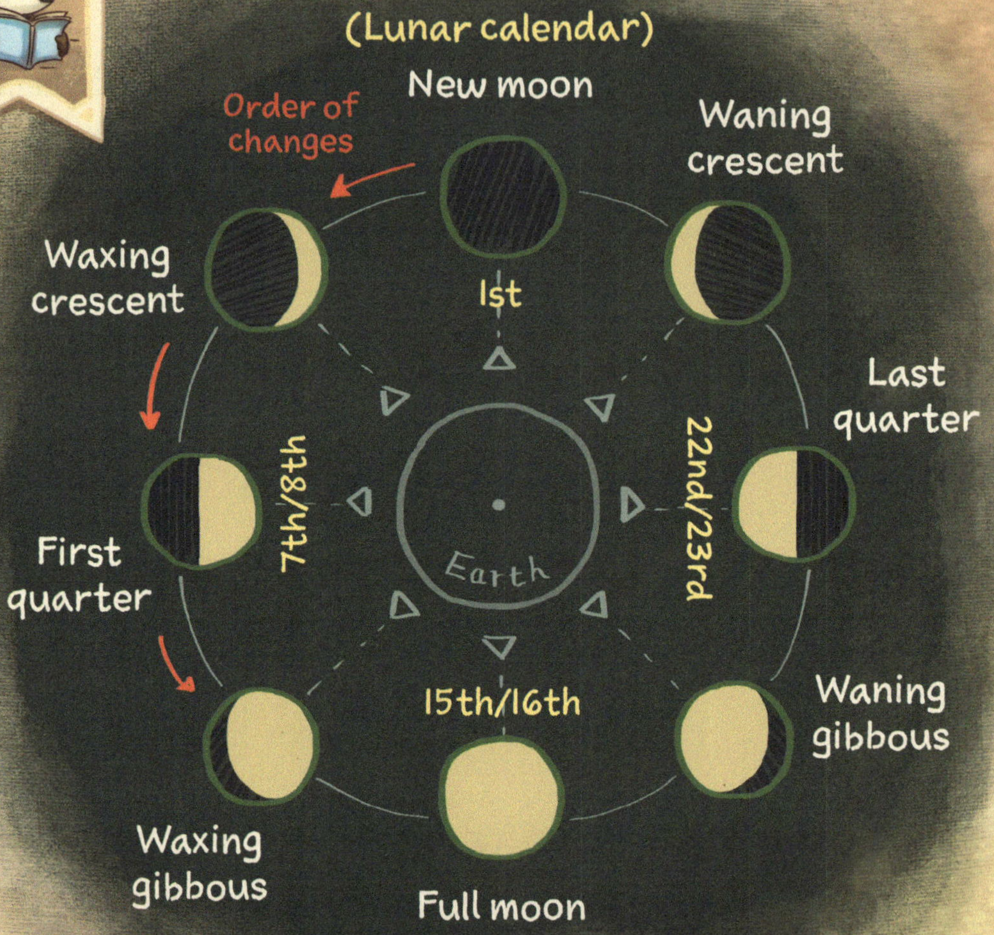

The moon will gradually change from a crescent to a full moon, then slowly change back to a crescent moon, repeating this cycle repeatedly. The time it takes for the moon to complete this change is called "a month."

What traditional festivals are there during the full moon?

Festival lantern

Lantern Festival

the 15th day of the first lunar month

Also known as the Shangyuan Festival, originated from the ancient custom of lighting lanterns and praying for blessings among the common people.

Ghost Festival

the 15th day of the seventh lunar month

The origin of this festival can be traced back to the worship of ancestors in ancient times, and its cultural connotation is to respect and be filial to ancestors.

River lantern

Mid-Autumn Festival

the 15th day of the eighth lunar month

This festival originated from worshipping celestial phenomena and evolved from the ancient sacrificial activity of "offering sacrifice to the moon in the Mid-Autumn."

Osmanthus wine

In which positio below is the moon invisible from earth?

Hint: On a clear night, which moon position cannot be seen from earth? What time of the month is it?

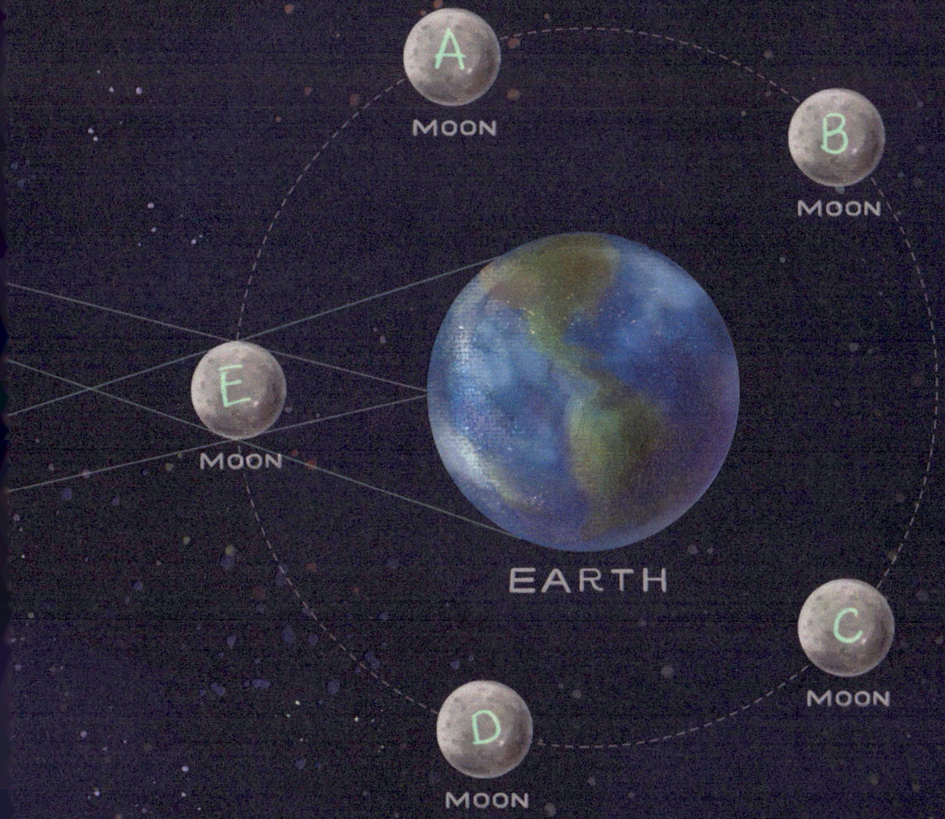

A solar eclipse occurs during the new moon;
a lunar eclipse occurs during the full moon.

Chapter 4

The Strange Instrument

Location: Earth Weather: Cloudy to fine

When I came to my senses, the carriage had already disappeared into the crowd. The street was so crowded that I had to use all my strength to walk a few meters. It was impossible to catch up with the carriage, and I was so anxious that I stamped my feet.

“Little Fox, don’t worry, wait for me here; I’ll look . . .”

Suddenly, Yolk Pie "swooshed" out of my backpack and flew toward the direction of the carriage.

I anxiously waited in place, no longer interested in the beautiful lanterns, just hoping for the Yolk Pie to return soon. But after a long time, there was still no sign of the Yolk Pie. I forced myself to relax, and before I knew it, my eyelids slowly began to droop, and I fell asleep again . . .

"Little Fox, Little Fox! Wake up!"

I heard a shout and opened my eyes to see a yellow ball in front of me. At first, I thought it was a lantern, but on closer inspection, it turned out to be the Yolk Pie.

"Yolk Pie, you're finally back!" I rubbed my eyes and realized that it was already dawn.

"They've taken the spaceship to the **EASTERN HOLY TEMPLE**!"

"The Eastern Holy Temple?"

Yolk Pie brought me to a magnificent PALACE. The golden glass tiles shimmered in the sunlight.

"This is it!"

Yolk Pie led me through the palace, and we found many small and large palaces behind it, each layered on top of another, and they all looked similar.

"This place is too big, and there are too many palaces. Where are they going to put the spaceship? Are we going to have to search through all the palaces?" I asked.

At this moment, a hoarse voice came from nearby—

"Sunshine! Sunshine!"

Yolk Pie and I ran over and saw a strange old man muttering to himself. In front of him was a flat stone tablet with a SCALE, and a tall pole stood straight on it.

The eccentric old man would look up at the sun for a moment, then lower his head to look at the shadow of the rod on the slate, then record something on the paper while muttering to himself. He looked very busy.

"What is that thing?" I pointed to the strange instrument and asked Yolk Pie for advice.

"That slate lying flat on the ground is called '*gui*' [圭], and the vertical rod is called '*biao*' [表]. When combined, people can infer the time based on the length of the shadow of the *biao* at noon every day," Yolk Pie explained.

"So, you can know the time based on the length of the shadow?" I still needed to understand what principle the strange instrument was using.

Yolk Pie told me that the height of the sun at NOON changes **REGULARLY** every day. The day with the longest shadow of the *biao* at noon is the winter solstice, and the day with the shortest shadow of the *biao* at noon is the summer solstice. The interval between two winter solstices is one year.

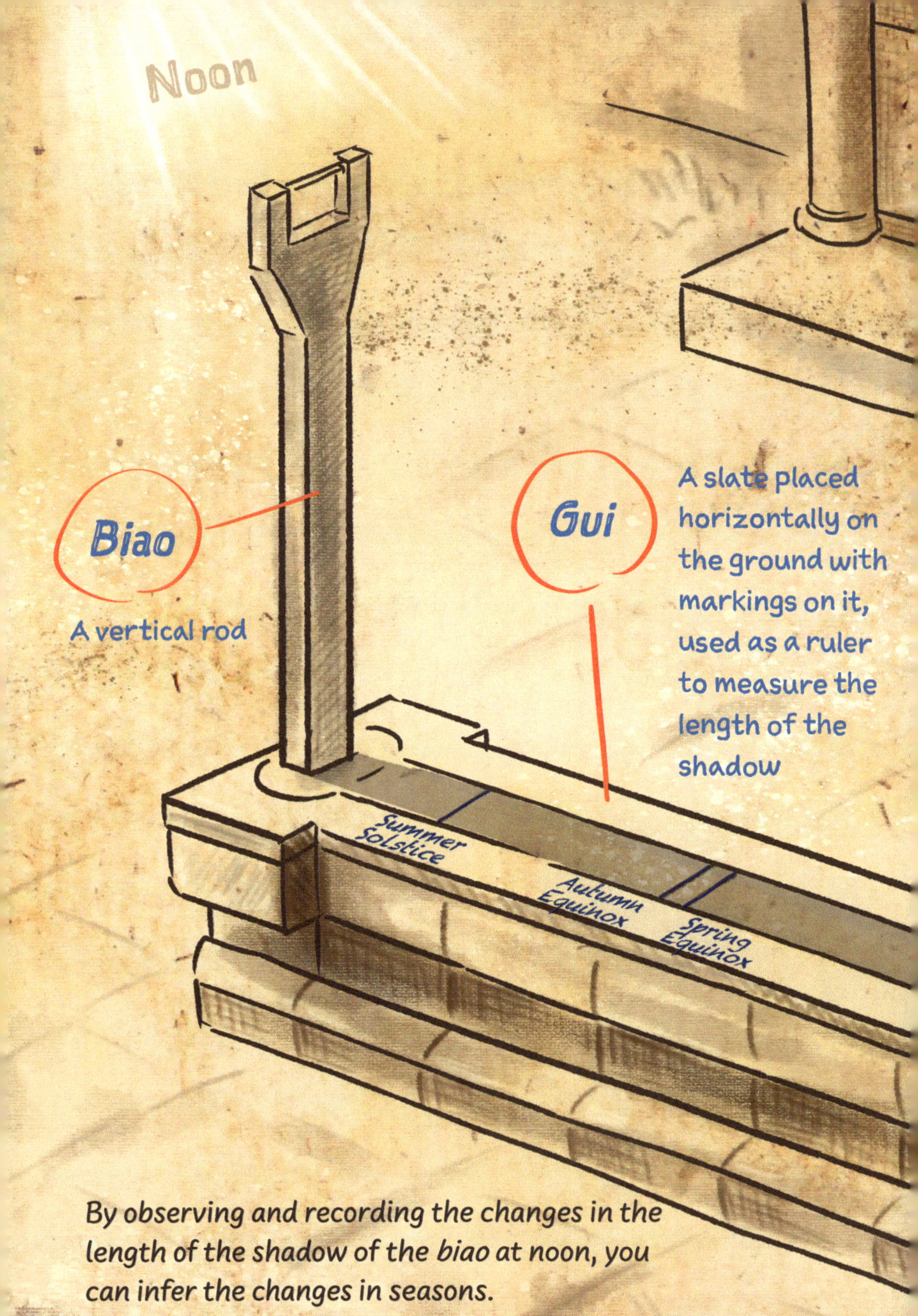

By observing and recording the changes in the length of the shadow of the biao *at noon, you can infer the changes in seasons.*

?
Winter Solstice
North

I was curious and about to take a closer look at the strange instrument, but Yolk Pie grabbed my hat from behind.

"Little Fox, let's go find the spaceship quickly."

I suppressed my curiosity and walked along the palace wall with Yolk Pie.

After walking for a while, we heard **WHISPERS** coming from the other side of the palace wall:

"Hey, have you heard?"

"What?"

"A divine object fell from the sky and was transported to our Eastern Holy Temple last night."

"Are you talking about what was taken to Mount Penglai?"

"Shh . . . lower your voice . . ."

Yolk Pie and I looked at each other. Could the divine object they were talking about be my spaceship? Before I could figure it out, a eunuch ran and shouted:

"Something's wrong! Something's wrong! Mount Penglai is on fire! Hurry up and put out the fire! Hurry up and put out the fire!"

Mount Penglai? If the spaceship was there, it would be in danger! I couldn't help but feel nervous.

"Yolk Pie, let's go take a look!"

Yolk Pie flew up high, and we followed the crowd of firefighters to the edge of an artificial lake. There were three islands in the center of the lake, and one of them was emitting billowing black smoke, surrounded by boats fighting the fire.

"That island on fire should be the Mount Penglai they were talking about!"

I quickly jumped onto a boat by the lake, and with the help of Yolk Pie, we soon arrived at the small island called Mount Penglai.

Through the rolling thick smoke on the island, I vaguely saw something with a familiar outline.

"Right, it's a spaceship!"

I was extremely excited. My previous speculation was correct. I quickly wet my clothes, covered my mouth and nose, and followed Yolk Pie's guidance to climb through the thick smoke. Soon, we successfully entered the spaceship.

Although there were many firefighters around the small island, the fire did not decrease but grew bigger and bigger! In no time, the raging fire surrounded the spaceship!

"Cough, cough, cough, cough . . . Let's leave here first, save the spaceship first!"

Although I covered my mouth and nose with wet clothes, I still inhaled a small amount of thick smoke. As I coughed, I reached out and pressed the spaceship's time-travel button . . .

Knowledge Secret

One Year and 24 Solar Terms

Through observation, people found that the sun does not rise from the same position daily but cycles within a specific range.

South   Changes in the Position of the Sun at Sunrise   North

On the day when the sun rises from the southernmost position on the horizon, at noon, the sun's height is the lowest, and the length of the pole's shadow is the longest. On this day, the daytime is the shortest, and the nighttime is the longest. The Northern Hemisphere is in the cold winter season, so this day is called the **WINTER SOLSTICE**.

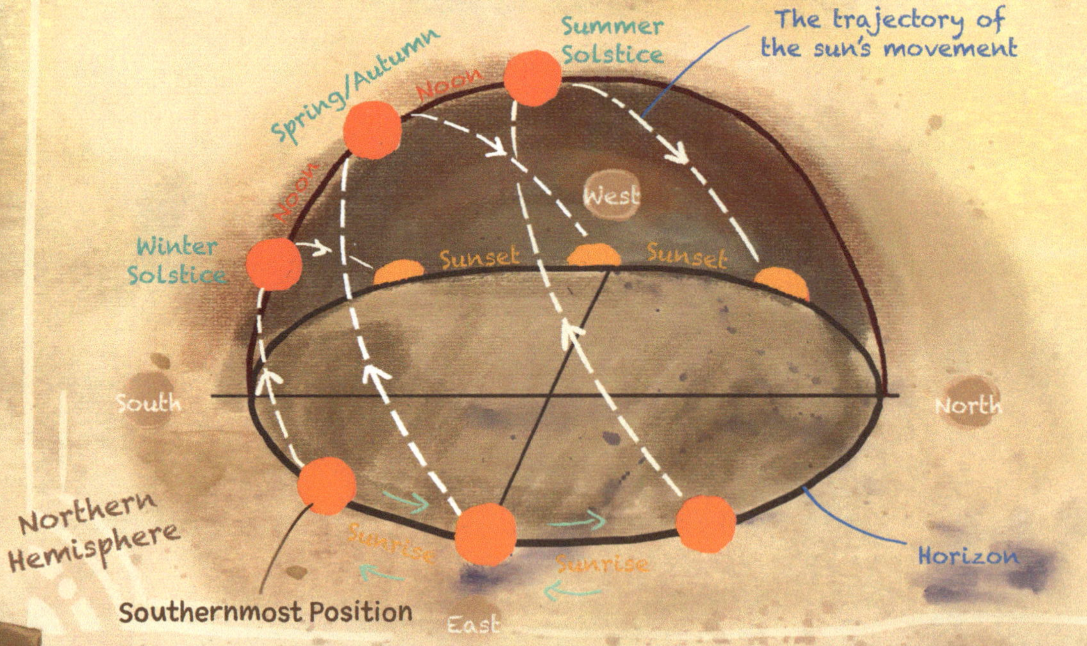

The ancients discovered the above rules through long-term observations and called the time interval between two winter solstices **A YEAR.**

Why not use the summer solstice?

By observing the length of the *gui*'s shadow at noon, we can infer the time of the day in a year.

The limitations of the *gui* are very strong. It cannot be used to infer time at night, on cloudy or rainy days.

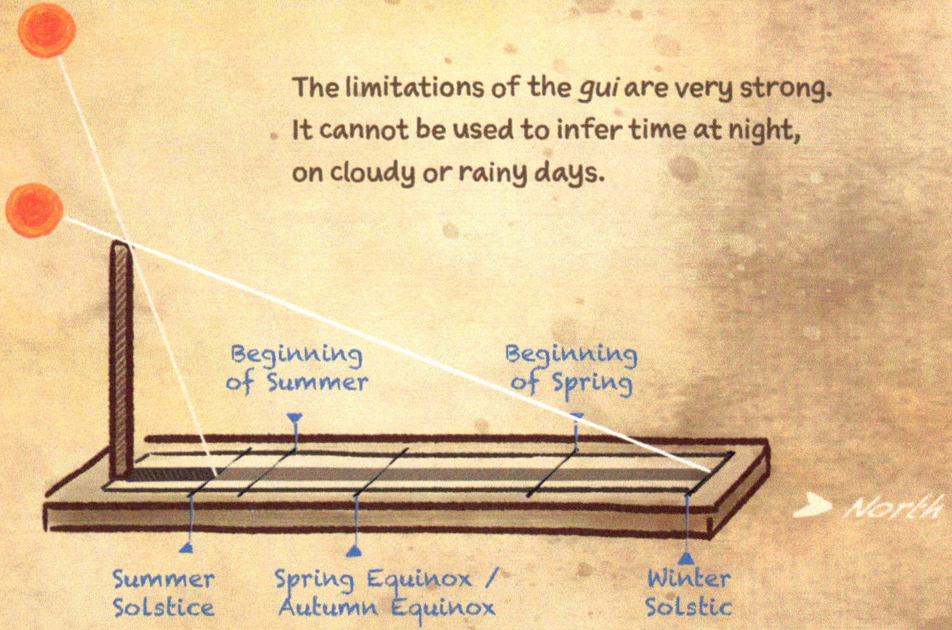

On the day of **WINTER SOLSTICE**, the sun's height at noon is **THE LOWEST**, and the length of the shadow is **THE LONGEST**.

On the day of **SUMMER SOLSTICE**, the sun's height at noon is **THE HIGHEST**, and the length of the shadow is **THE SHORTEST**.

SPRING EQUINOX and **AUTUMN EQUINOX**: The length of the daytime and nighttime are equal.

Dividing the time between winter solstice, spring equinox, summer solstice, and autumn equinox into equal parts, we get the beginning of spring, summer, autumn, and winter.

Beginning of Spring (立春 [*li chun*]), Beginning of Summer (立夏 [*li xia*]), Beginning of Autumn (立秋 [*li qiu*]), and Beginning of Winter (立冬 [*li dong*]): *the solar terms used by the ancients to divide the four seasons.*

The word "立" (*li*) *means "beginning," and* "立春" (*li chun*) *means spring begins on this day.*

With these eight solar terms, people divided every two into three equal parts, thus giving rise to the 24 solar terms.

THE 24 SOLAR TERMS result from Chinese people's wisdom derived from their long-term observation and labor and an important discovery in the history of world astronomy. Today, it is still useful as a guide for agricultural production.

Taosi Ancient Observatory

This ancient observatory is located in Xiangfen County, Linfen City, Shanxi Province, China, and it is composed of 13 pillars, 12 observation slits, and 1 observation point.

This is the earliest known observatory in the world to date.

By observing the sun's position at sunrise through the slit from the observation point, one could determine the solar term of the day.

From which narrow slit can you see the sunrise on the day of Spring Equinox and Autumn Equinox?

Hint:
Winter solstice can be observed through the second narrow slit.
Summer solstice can be observed through the twelfth narrow slit.
The first narrow slit does not have the function of observing sunrise.

Chapter 5

A Clock Made of Water?

Location: Earth   Weather: Cloudy

In the blink of an eye, we found ourselves in another place. The road here had neatly trimmed small pine trees and rock gardens on both sides, and a **TRIUMPHAL ARCH** with three archways stood in the middle of the road. The center archway was arched, and the slightly smaller archways on either side were rectangular. The door was decorated with various patterns and carvings, which were very exquisite. There were also two low walls on either side of the gate, alternately colored yellow and green.

I turned around and looked at Yolk Pie, puzzled. "Yolk Pie, where are we?"

"This looks like a royal garden. It feels familiar," Yolk Pie answered slowly.

"Oh? Familiar? Is your home nearby, then?" I asked quickly.

"No."

Yolk Pie's tone was very certain, which **DISAPPOINTED ME GREATLY.**

"Since you feel familiar here, let's look at the pavilion. We can see farther from a higher place!" I pointed to the gazebo on a small hill in the distance.

The small hill didn't look high, but the road up the hill wound around. When we reached the top, I was sweating profusely and sat on the steps before the gazebo, gasping for breath.

Xianfa
Mountain?

Luoshi
Archway

This was an octagonal gazebo with a double eave roof, and the patterns on the pavilion were finely carved. While resting, I carefully looked around.

"Little Fox, there's a fountain below the mountain. Let's have a look," Yolk Pie said.

After speaking, Yolk Pie flew down the mountain, and I still needed to warm up my seat! Yolk Pie was never so enthusiastic before. Did it remember something? I quickly got up and followed.

We passed several small fountains and buildings and came to a large fountain. In the pool's center was a large shell with 6 bronze statues of human-headed beasts on each side arranged in the shape of the Chinese character "八," the number 8.

"Why do these statues have human bodies and animal heads?" I asked.

Yolk Pie didn't answer me. It circled the fountain and muttered quietly:

"Rat, ox, tiger, rabbit, dragon, snake, horse, goat, monkey, rooster, dog, pig . . ."

"Hey, Yolk Pie, what are you muttering about? Did you remember something?" I looked at Yolk Pie in confusion.

"This is **THE CHINESE ZODIAC ANIMALS BRONZE HEADS FOUNTAIN**. Every **12 EARTHLY BRANCHES**, the bronze heads take turns spraying water. We will know the time when we see different animal heads spraying water."

At last, Yolk Pie spoke normally again, and I breathed a sigh of relief. But what connected the Zodiac Animals and the 12 earthly branches?

Yolk Pie told me that each Zodiac Animal corresponds to a specific earthly branch, which is related to the habits and characteristics of that particular animal. For example, the period from 11:00 a.m. to 1:00 p.m. is when the sunlight is the strongest, and the "*yang qi*" (energy) is most abundant. Most animals rest lying down during this time, but horses are most active. That's why the ancients used **HORSES TO INDICATE NOON**.

In the ancient battle, soldiers looked at the head of the general's horse to decide whether to advance or retreat. Later, it refers to following someone's action.

The bronze horse head spouted water, followed by the other eleven animals.

"Wow, it's so beautiful!" I was so excited that I opened my eyes wide.

"The 12 bronze heads only spout water together at noon. This fountain is a **HYDRAULIC CLOCK**, based on the same principle as a **COPPER CLEPSYDRA**."

"Huh? Copper clepsydra? What is this?"

"It's a kind of clock made with water, indicating time based on the amount of water dripping," Yolk Pie patiently explained.

"Oh." I didn't understand, but I was captivated by the impressive sight before me. Then I noticed a particularly unusual statue with antlers on its head, long whiskers on its mouth, a neck resembling a snake, and fish scales covering its body.

"What animal is this, Yolk Pie?"

I turned to look at Yolk Pie, who was staring blankly at the statue with trembling excitement.

"Yolk Pie?" I called softly.

"Dragon!" Yolk Pie exclaimed in a quivering voice. "I remember now! I was born in the year of the dragon!"

"Haha, that's great! That's great! We can finally send you home!" I exclaimed with excitement.

"However," Yolk Pie said softly, "I don't remember the exact date. Many years have been the year of the dragon . . ."

"What? So, we can only send you home if we know the exact year you were born?" I asked.

"Yes," Yolk Pie nodded.

Knowledge Secret

Copper Clepsydra

The copper clepsydra, known as the louke (water clock) or the dripping pot, is an ancient timer.

1 Water-releasing single pot

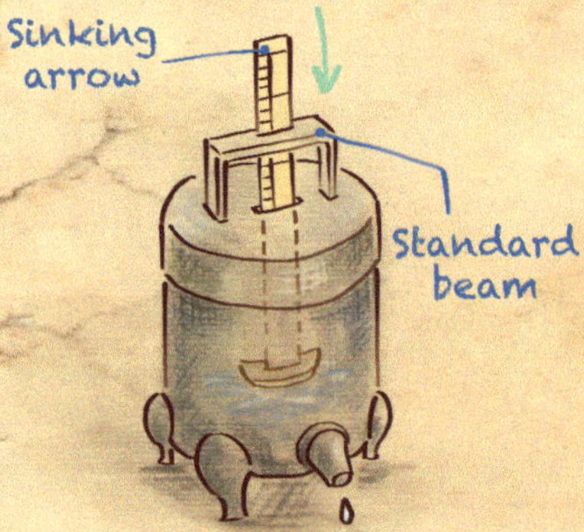

There is a **SINKING ARROW** with graduations inside the pot, where different graduations correspond to different times. Water in the pot drips out from the lower side of the pot. As the water leaks, the arrow sinks. The **STANDARD BEAM** on the top of the pot indicates the time.

In the early days, only one dripping pot was used, but the speed of water dripping was affected by the amount of water in the pot. If there was more water in the pot, the water would drip faster; if there was less water, the water would drip slower, causing errors in timing.

To solve this problem, people improved the multi-level dripping device, adopting the water-receiving method to measure time.

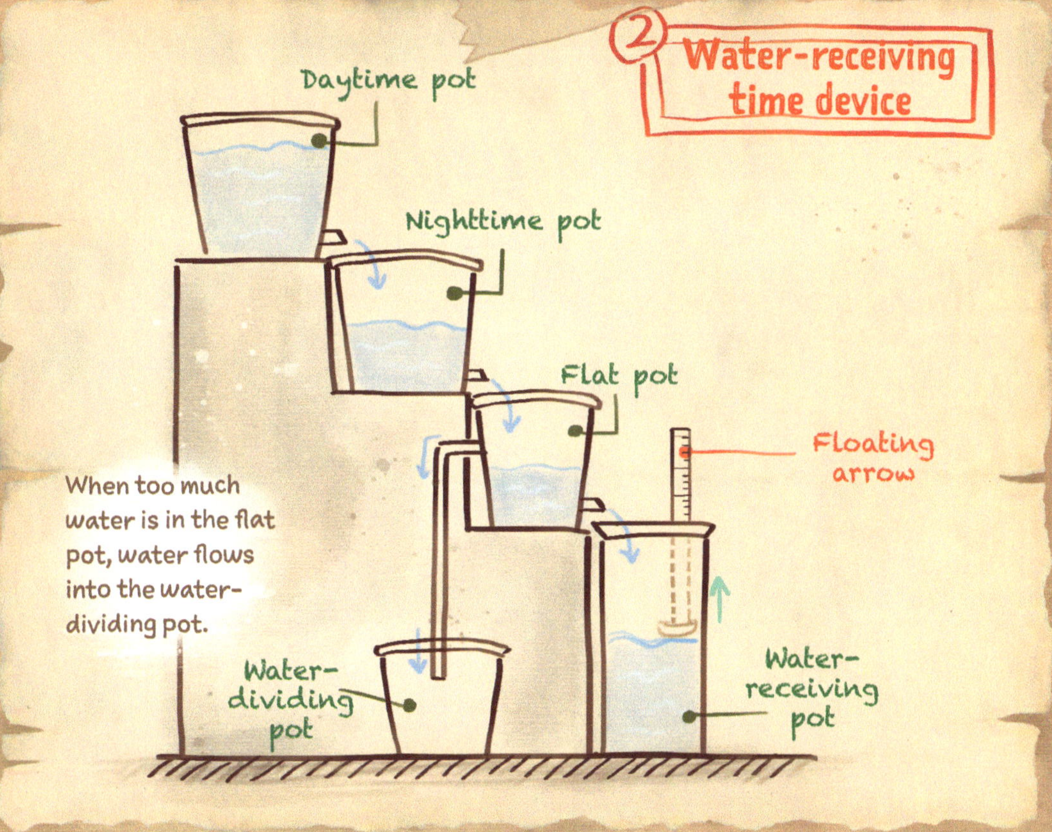

Water in the flat pot is supplied from the pot above, so the water in the flat pot can remain relatively constant, and the speed of water dripping into the water-receiving pot can remain constant. When the water level in the water-receiving pot rises, the arrow floats. As the **FLOATING ARROW** rises, people can read the time from the graduation marked on the arrow.

Whether using sinking or floating arrows, a day and night are divided into 96 quarters, recording 12 earthly branches in a day.

The 12 earthly branches are divided into 96 quarters. How many minutes is a quarter?

4
Challenge
Pig
Rooster
Goat
Snake
Rabbit
Ox
Earthly branch of hai (亥)
Earthly branch of you (酉)
Earthly branch of wei (未)
Earthly branch of si (巳)
Earthly branch of mao (卯)
Earthly branch of chou (丑)
Cool!
1 earthly branch equals 2 hours.

Chinese Zodiac Animals
Water clock fountain?
Rat
Tiger
Dragon
Horse
Monkey
Dog
Earthly branch of zi (子)
Earthly branch of yin (寅)
Earthly branch of chen (辰)
Earthly branch of wu (午)
Earthly branch of shen (申)
Earthly branch of xu (戌)
2024 is the Year of the Dragon.
Little Fox was born in 2018. What is his zodiac sign?

Chapter 6

Sun Clock

Location: Earth Weather: Cloudy to fine

As the excitement turned to disappointment, I slumped weakly against the fountain, and Yolk Pie fell silent with me . . .

After what felt like a long time, Yolk Pie finally spoke up.

"I think an astronomical clock might come in handy."

"An astronomical clock?" I perked up. "You can figure out the exact year you were born using an astronomical clock?"

"Although it's a bit complicated, it should be possible to deduce," Yolk Pie said, thinking as he spoke.

"Is there an astronomical clock here?"

Just then, we heard a faint "**JINGLE, JINGLE**" sound in the distance. Yolk Pie and I exchanged glances, but before I could say anything, Yolk Pie flew off toward the sound.

Was that sound coming from an astronomical clock? Or did Yolk Pie remember something else? Is there an astronomical clock here?

I followed Yolk Pie, running behind him with questions in my head.

After a while, the "jingle, jingle" sound suddenly stopped. Yolk Pie suddenly came to a halt, hovering in mid-air. I was too busy running ahead to react, and almost bumped into Yolk Pie's bottom! It wasn't until I snapped out of my daze that I noticed we had arrived at a magical place.

Palaces of all sizes stood neatly on white marble platforms in the water, with roofs made of glass tiles in shades of yellow, green, and blue. The glass tiles **SPARKLED** in the sunlight, and the reflection on the lake **SHIMMERED** like a **MYTHICAL FAIRYLAND**.

The scenery before me was enchanting . . . Suddenly, I saw something strange in front of the palace!

It was a stone column over a person's height, with a tilted stone disc on top . . .

"Yolk Pie, what's that?"

"A sun clock," Yolk Pie blurted out.

"A sun clock?"

I was full of doubt and curiosity as I ran over to examine it closely. The sun clock looked strange, with the dial divided into 24 equal parts with no numbers but 12 Chinese characters in a circle. Even stranger, there were no hands on the clock, only a copper needle sticking straight into the center.

"Are you sure this is a 'clock'?" I asked skeptically.

Yolk Pie flew over, thought for a moment, and said, "To be exact, it should be called a '**SUNDIAL**.'"

"A sundial? What's that? How is it related to a clock?" I asked.

"Haha!" Yolk Pie laughed. "A sundial is an instrument to tell time by observing the sun's shadow. When the sun shines on the copper needle, it will cast a shadow on the stone disc. As the sun moves, the shadow will fall on different parts of the dial, and wherever the shadow of the needle falls, it represents the time . . ."

The Yolk Pie kept talking non-stop.

Sundial needle
Sundial plate
Base

I tiptoed and looked at the stone plate. The sunlight shone on the green copper needle, and its shadow fell on the grid on the stone plate as expected. But I still had doubts: Why was the stone plate tilted? Wouldn't it be easier to observe if placed flat on the ground? And why were there 24 grids on the stone plate, but only 12 Chinese characters were carved?

Just then, "jingle, jingle" floated into my ears from behind.

"Yolk Pie! Listen!" However, the Yolk Pie didn't hear anything. I had a strong hunch that the sound was related to the astronomical clock!

I turned around and ran to the palace behind me, pressed my ear against the door, and was about to listen carefully. "CREAK"—I accidentally pushed open the door, stumbled, and almost fell. I saw a tall statue directly opposite the door, with stairs on both sides leading up to it. The sound came from above the stairs!

I climbed the stairs stealthily and peeked out from the stairwell.

"Wow! Yolk Pie, look!"

The room had clock models with novel shapes, such as pavilions, pagodas, locomotives, carriages, animals, plants, etc. Some were super large, some were very small, and none were the same.

On these gorgeous clocks, there were acrobats performing, birds singing softly, flowers blooming beautifully, vehicles shuttling back and forth, and various animals with movable eyes, which were **INGENIOUS** and **MAGNIFICENT**, making people **DAZZLED**!

The Yolk Pie and I were deeply shocked by the clocks in front of us. Because we were so absorbed in admiring them that we didn't even notice someone approaching.

"Who's there? Don't move!" A soldier yelled.

The sudden shout frightened me, and my instinct was to run away.

After running two steps, I realized that the Yolk Pie hadn't followed me and was still dazed. Without thinking, I hugged the Yolk Pie tightly, then ran madly down the stairs.

The soldiers behind me chased after me closely, and the surrounding voices became increasingly noisy. Suddenly, more soldiers were chasing us!

I didn't have time to think about the consequences of being caught, so I held my breath and, relying on my memory, ran to where the spaceship was parked.

Finally, I ran into the spaceship with the Yolk Pie in my arms. I gasped for breath and saw the soldiers surrounding the spaceship. I quickly reached for the time travel button—

"Wait!" The Yolk Pie suddenly shouted, "2036! Let's go to the year 2036!"

Apart from gasping, I couldn't make any sound, so I nodded at the Yolk Pie and entered the year it said, then pressed the spaceship's time travel button immediately . . .

Knowledge Secret

What is 日晷 (sundial)?

"日" (*ri*) is the sun, and "晷" (*gui*) is the shadow of the sun.

The sun shines on the sundial needle; it will leave a shadow on the sundial surface. The scale engraved on the sundial surface is called the "sundial degree." As the sun's position moves, the shadow of the needle falls on a different scale, and the time can be determined by the scale where the shadow of the needle is located.

Common sundials can be broadly classified into three categories.

(1) Ground sundial:

The sundial is placed flat on the ground.

(2) Vertical sundial:

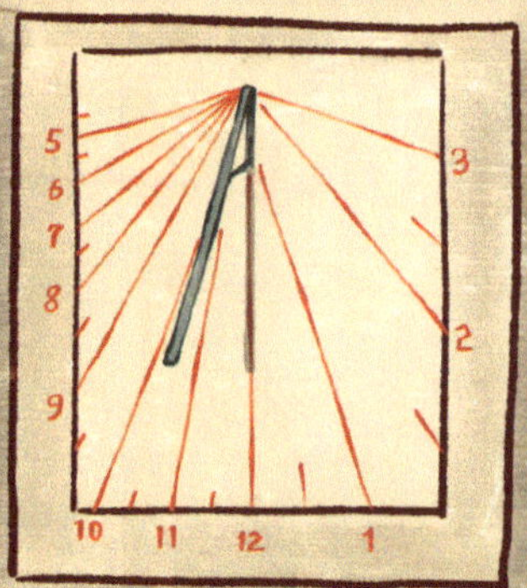

The sundial surface is perpendicular to the floor and is usually se into the wall.

(3) Equatorial sundial:

The sundial surface is parallel to the equator.

The timing of the indication is relatively accurate, and the length of the needle shadow is largely unaffected by the sun's altitude.

Sundial needle

A copper needle is inserted vertically in the sundial's center, parallel to earth axis, and the upper end of the sundial needle points to the North Pole. The angles between the sundial needle and the base and the sundial plate tilt angle are the same.

Sundial plate

stone disc, parallel to the equator, tilted at an angle that varies depending on its location.

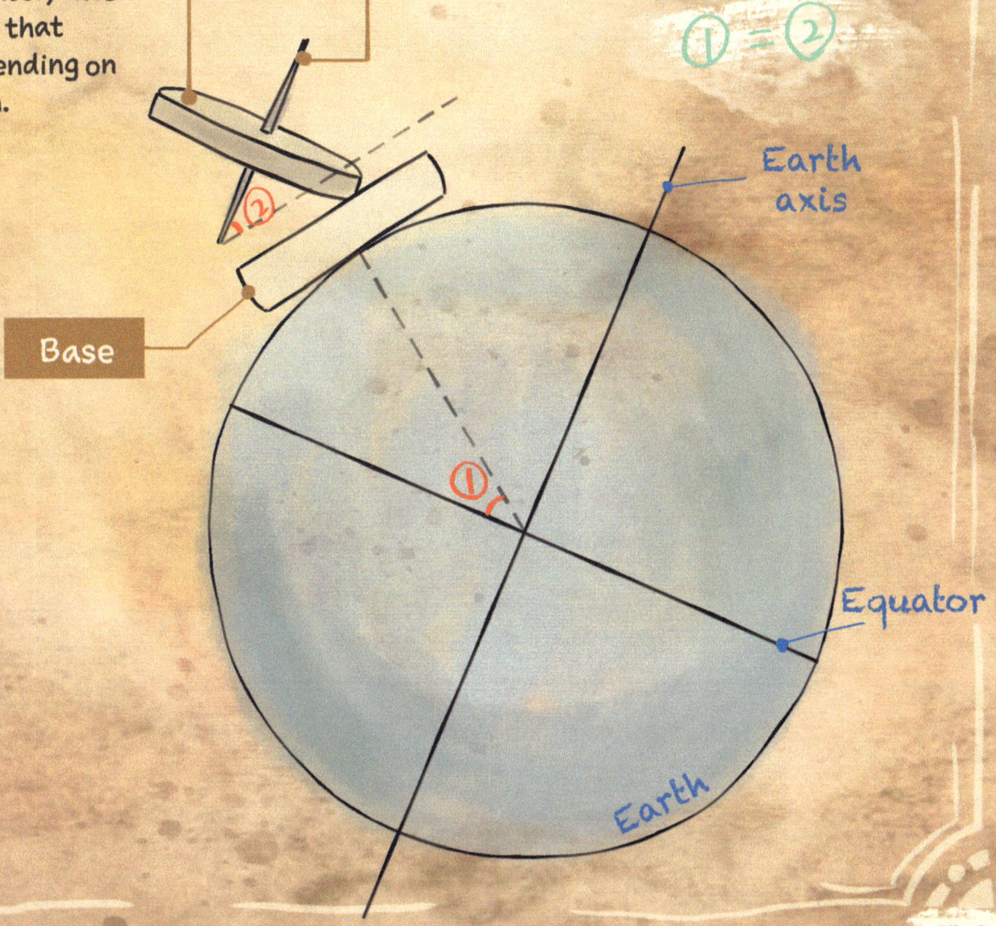

5 Challenge

What time is it in another hour?

Observe the position of the shadow of the sundial needle in the diagram and guess where the shadow of the needle will fall in another hour.

An inch of time is an inch of gold; an inch of gold cannot buy an inch of time. "An inch of time" is the time consumed by the shadow of the sundial needle changing one inch on the sundial plate.

The passage of time follows the movement of the heavens, and the four seasons succeed one another.

Hint:
The sun moves in the direction from A to B.
One earthly branch is two hours.

Chapter 7

Direction

Location: Earth   Weather: Clear

In the blink of an eye, the spaceship traversed.

"Wow, we're here!" Yolk Pie and I eagerly ran down the spaceship and faced a celestial pool. The blue pool water was like a huge mirror, reflecting the blue sky, white clouds, green mountains, and trees.

"Little Fox . . . this . . . doesn't seem like my home . . ."

"What?" I couldn't believe my ears when Yolk Pie said this. "That's impossible! I set the time correctly!" Could it be . . . I suddenly realized and slapped my head, "Could it be that the time on the spaceship's system is different from the time on earth?"

What should we do? Lost in thought, I was suddenly interrupted by a tap on my shoulder. "Ouch, Yolk Pie, stop it!"

"What? Ouch!" Yolk Pie was also hit for no reason and made a crisp metallic sound.

I turned around and saw several **MONKEYS** on the vines behind us, throwing stones at us. I didn't care about them, but they became even more aggressive, continuously throwing stones at the ground and the spaceship.

I quickly covered my head with my hand and took a few steps toward the direction of the forest, waving my hand to scare them away. "Get out! Get out!" I didn't expect them to become even more excited when I yelled at them.

"Yolk Pie, you protect the spaceship, and I'll distract them!" I picked up a stone and ran toward the monkeys.

"FIRST, CATCH THE RINGLEADER. The one with the raised tail is the monkey king!" Yolk Pie shouted behind me.

I looked up and saw a monkey with a raised tail giving orders. I used all my strength to throw the stone at the monkey king who bared his teeth. Angry, he signaled several monkeys to run away, and they quickly disappeared without a trace.

"Hmph, let's see if you dare to be so arrogant now!" I patted the sand on my hands, feeling proud. But then, I realized that I had unknowingly run into a tropical forest while chasing the monkeys, and to make matters worse, there were SEVERAL FORKS IN THE ROAD behind me! I was so focused on chasing the monkeys that I didn't notice which path I had come from . . .

"Yolk Pie . . . Yolk Pie . . ." I shouted twice at the top of my lungs, but besides the sound of birds, I didn't get any response . . .

①
②
③
④
?

"I don't think I've run too far, right? Otherwise, let me try to walk back." My heartbeat was fast, and I unconsciously walked to a huge tree. The tree had huge roots and a thick trunk that would require more than ten people holding hands to surround it!

I saw countless branches stretching out from the trunk, bending and curving through the dense leaves, reaching the sky. I couldn't see the end of it. It was like a **TREE THAT COULD LEAD TO THE SKY**!

"Just now, did I pass through here?" I tried hard to recall if I had passed through here and sat on the thick tree roots. After resting for a while, I suddenly **HAD AN IDEA**!

"Right, if I leave some marks where I passed by, it can find me when Yolk Pie sees them! Haha!"

So, as I walked, I left marks on the tree, the ground, and the forks in the road.

After walking for a while, I found strange-looking plants around me with rows of **CURVED FRUITS**.

Some had yellow skin; some had green skin. I picked one of the boat-shaped fruits and sniffed it closely. A sweet fragrance hit my face. Just as I was wondering if I could eat this fruit, Yolk Pie's voice suddenly came from behind me—

"This is a banana, and it can replenish energy."

"Yolk Pie!" I exclaimed with joy. "Did you see the marks I left?"

Yolk Pie nodded. "I also saw the stones and broken plants on the ground."

"Wow!" I took a bite of the "BANANA" fruit and suddenly remembered, "By the way, you came to find me; what about my spaceship? How is it?"

"Don't worry. The spaceship is safe."

Hearing Yolk Pie say this, I breathed a sigh of relief and finally tasted the sweetness of the banana.

After resting for a while, we continued to walk back. Yolk Pie led the way in front of me, saying we needed to go north to get back.

"How do you tell directions? I can't tell directions in the forest," I couldn't help but ask my question.

"The sun rises in the east and sets in the west. We can roughly determine the east-west direction based on the direction of the sun's movement, and then the north-south direction is also determined," Yolk Pie explained.

"Haha! I know, up is north, down is south, left is west, and right is east!" I blurted out.

The sun slowly set, and the sky began to show scattered stars. Although Yolk Pie could emit light, its light appeared particularly weak in the forest.

"Huh? Yolk Pie, your flying speed seems to have increased." I had to jog to keep up with it.

"Uh . . . I . . . I . . . I just want to get back to the spaceship faster . . ." Yolk Pie said awkwardly.

"But now there is no sun. How do you know this direction is north?"

"With the POLARIS to guide us, we will not lose our way."

Looking up at the night sky, I exclaimed, "Wow, there are so many stars here! Which one is the Polaris?"

The Yolk Pie slowed and said, "First, you must find the BIG DIPPER, which looks like a spoon made of stars. Then, there is a brighter star close to the mouth of the spoon, the Polaris!"

"Wow, the brightest star in the night sky will guide us, ha-ha!"

However, just as I was enjoying the stars, Yolk Pie was suddenly knocked to the side by a fierce beast with two glowing green eyes.

Fortunately, Yolk Pie could fly, and the fierce beast missed its pounce. As I was happy for Yolk Pie, the fierce beast turned its head and stared at me with ferocious eyes!

Clouded leopard

The clouded leopard's limbs are short and agile, and its tail is as long as its body. Its body is golder with large dark cloud-shaped spots. This leopard sleeps on tree during the day and hunts at dawr dusk, and night.

RUN!

"Little Fox, run!" Yolk Pie shouted above my head.

"T-t-t-tiger?" My legs went weak, and my body trembled uncontrollably.

"Not a tiger, a clouded leopard, run!" Yolk Pie battled the leopard in mid-air to buy me time to escape. I stumbled a few steps and fell into the water with a "**SPLASH**"! The water flowed rapidly, and I was carried away far!

"Yolk Pie! Yolk Pie!" I shouted. The leopard paced along the bank but did not follow me into the water, which relieved me.

"Little Fox, hold onto that tree trunk!" The Yolk Pie shouted above my head.

With the faint light emitted by Yolk Pie, I saw a tree trunk extending into the water ahead of me, and I swam toward it with all my strength. However, when I touched the trunk, I realized **SOMETHING WAS WRONG**!

This was an old, withered tree with an almost hollow trunk. Before fully embracing it, I heard a "CRACK" sound, and the trunk broke! I continued to drift downstream with the broken trunk, and the water flow seemed to be getting faster and faster!

"Oh no! There's a waterfall ahead!" Yolk Pie stood in front of the trunk, and although my drifting speed slowed, the water continued pushing us forward!

Suddenly, I felt my body flying up, falling, down, down . . .

"Splash!" I fell into the water again.

I struggled to float to the surface, but the strong force of the waterfall pressed me deep under the water, and I choked on the water, feeling like I was about to suffocate. Just before I lost consciousness, in a daze, I saw a huge black shadow swimming toward me, holding me up to the surface . . .

Knowledge Secret

Can stars help us identify directions?

Ancient people observed the starry sky at night and found that the stars were constantly moving, but one star remained "still," and that was Polaris.

The Polaris appears not to move because it is aligned with earth axis, and its position almost never changes due to its rotation. Therefore, people often use the Polaris to identify directions.

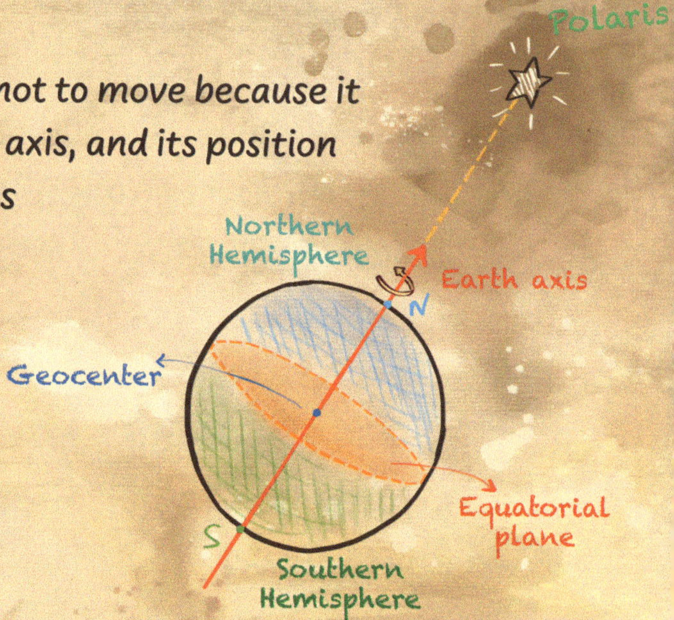

Try it out:

Stand in one place under light and spin around, observing the position of the light above your head and the changing position of other objects around you.

You will find that the position of the light above your head does not change, while the objects around you appear to be rotating.

Through observing the stars, ancient people also discovered the rules of seasonal changes (a result of earth's rotation).

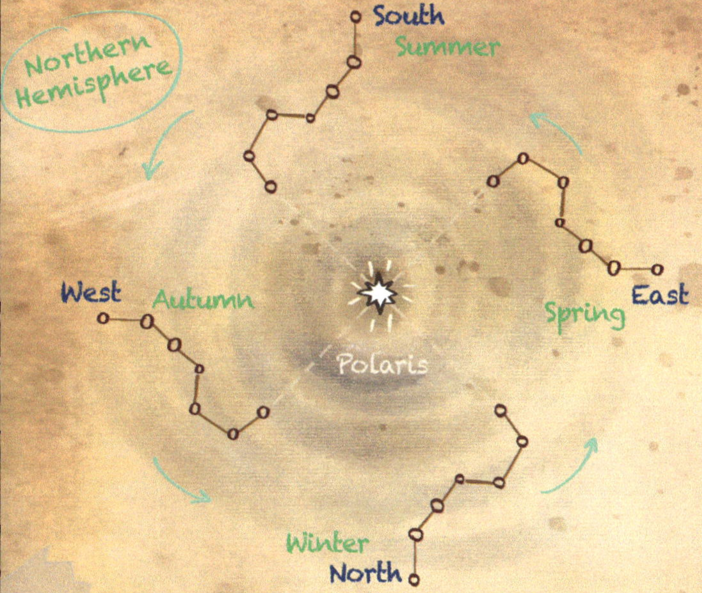

When the handle of the Big Dipper points east, the world is in spring;
When the handle of the Big Dipper points south, the world is in summer;
When the handle of the Big Dipper points west, the world is in autumn;
When the handle of the Big Dipper points north, the world is in winter.

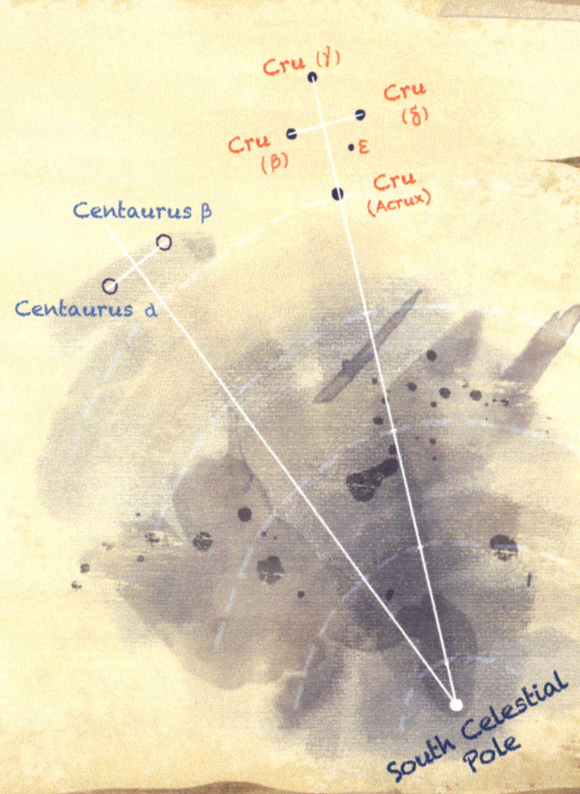

In many countries in Southern Hemisphere, people cannot see the Polaris, but they can see the Crux, which can also indicate direction. Therefore, the flags of countries such as Australia, New Zealand, Brazil, Papua New Guinea, and Samoa all feature the Crux.

6
Challenge
Aquarius
Capricorn
Sagittarius
(East) Azure Dragon
Phecda γ
Megrez δ
Alioth ε
Alkaid η
Mizar ζ
Scorpio
15
13
8
Libra
(South)
Vermilion Bird
North
East
South
West
Virgo

Which star in the picture is Polaris?

Hint: First, find the Big Dipper, then find the two stars at the front of the Dipper's handle, draw a line between them, and extend this line about five times its length. You will find Polaris.

Vaguely, I was lifted by a huge black shadow . . .
Hard and thick carapace
Tail

Limbs like paddles, capable of paddling in the water

Chapter 8

Compass

Location: Earth   Weather: Fine to cloudy, with scattered thunderstorms

"Yuck! So salty!" I spat out the salty seawater and struggled to sit up.

"Yolk Pie? Yolk Pie?" I shouted anxiously and soon saw a yellow ball not far away, which stood out on the white sandy beach.

Yolk Pie was lying face down with its butt in the air, half buried in the sand. I vaguely saw a string of numbers written under its butt, so I quickly looked closer. But suddenly, Yolk Pie flew up into the air.

"Ah, ah, I'm suffocating!"

"Yolk Pie! Yolk Pie! We're saved!" I shouted with joy. "But who saved us?"

Yolk Pie shook its head. "I don't know. I automatically entered sleep mode after falling into the water."

Just as I was about to say something, I suddenly remembered that we needed to return to our spaceship. "Yolk Pie, which way should we go now? Which direction is the spaceship in?"

"To the northwest," Yolk Pie replied, "but we're on another small island now."

"What? Another small island?" I exclaimed in surprise.

"That means . . . the spaceship . . . is not here?"

Looking around, we saw an ENDLESS sea all around us. It would be IMPOSSIBLE if we tried to swim to another island from here! I collapsed onto the sandy beach like a deflated ball, but Yolk Pie suddenly yelled, "Look, Little Fox!"

"A boat!" A boat was sailing toward us! I was so excited that tears almost sprang from my eyes, and I couldn't help but jump up and down. But then, 5, 10, 20 boats appeared on the sea . . .

In just a moment, hundreds of boats appeared on the sea! They were so densely packed that they looked like stars in the sky. We were both stunned and before we could even think about hiding, it was too late . . .

"Who are you? State your name! Why did you trespass into this forbidden area?" A mighty person stood on a huge ship, looking at us from above. He wore a black official hat and a white official gown and carried a treasure sword on his waist. He had a flaming red cloak behind him and looked IMPOSING and EXTRAORDINARY!

Who are you?
STATE YOUR NAME!
明

“Ah . . . we’re not . . . we’re just . . .” I was so nervous that I **COULDN’T SPEAK CLEARLY**, but before I could explain, Yolk Pie and I were forcibly taken aboard the ship . . .

“That’s what happened,” I explained the situation to the mighty commander of the fleet.

“So, you got lost?”

“Yes, yes!” I nodded quickly.

“I happen to know that place. I can take you there on the way.” The commander said casually.

I glanced at Yolk Pie and confirmed that I hadn’t misheard. To show my gratitude, I quickly pulled out a gold coin from my backpack that I got from Math Planet. However, the fleet commander waved his hand, saying, “No sweat.”

Suddenly, a soldier ran over quickly and reported, “Sir! A storm is approaching ahead. Please order a change of direction!”

This unexpected event made me worry again.

“If we change our course, can we still return?” I asked.

“Don’t worry.” The fleet commander approached a control panel and pointed to a dial with a pointer in the middle. There were 24 evenly divided characters around the edge of the dial.

“Is this a clock?” I asked curiously.

“No, it’s a compass!” said Yolk Pie beside me.

“Yes, with a compass, we don’t have to worry about getting lost.” The fleet commander gave the order, and the fleet changed its course, sailing away from where the storm was about to hit.

I leaned against the ship’s railing, letting the salty sea breeze blow on my face, and my body relaxed. I gently closed my eyes and immersed myself in the sound of the waves hitting and the crisp calls of seagulls overhead . . .

“Jingle, jingle . . .” Suddenly, there was a faint sound of the pointer hitting.

The sound came from the compass, and I looked at the dial and couldn't help but gasp—the pointer was turning left and right constantly! What's going on?

I immediately told the fleet commander about this discovery, but he remained calm and said, "The compass must have been **INTERFERED** with. It's okay. If we're lucky and there are no clouds at night, we can use the stars to determine the direction."

"What if we're not lucky?" I asked quickly.

"Then we'll keep sailing and exploring until it's sunny again . . ."

I didn't listen to what the fleet commander said after that. If we didn't return to the spaceship soon, who knows what other accidents might happen!

At this moment, Yolk Pie whispered, "Don't worry, I know the way."

Knowledge Secret

Why can a compass help us identify directions?

The earth we live on is a magnetic celestial body with two magnetic poles of opposite properties.

Earth's magnetic field is like a bar magnet inside earth, with the North Pole of the "bar magnet" pointing to earth's south magnetic pole and the South Pole of the "bar magnet" pointing to earth's north magnetic pole.

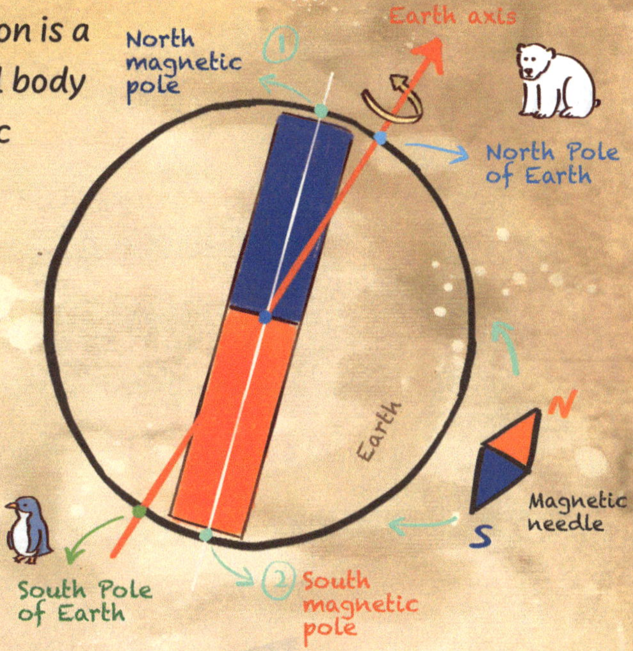

Magnetic north is south; magnetic south is north.

Development of the compass:

In China, people made natural magnets into spoon-shaped pointers, the ancient compass called "si nan" (司南).

Natural magnet

(1) *Si nan:*

Si nan—one of the Four Great Inventions of ancient China

(2) Water compass:

The magnetic needle floats freely on the water's surface to point direction, but the pointer of the water compass is easily influenced by wind and drifts.

(3) Non-floating compass:

The magnetic needle is supported by a copper nail to rotate freely without water.

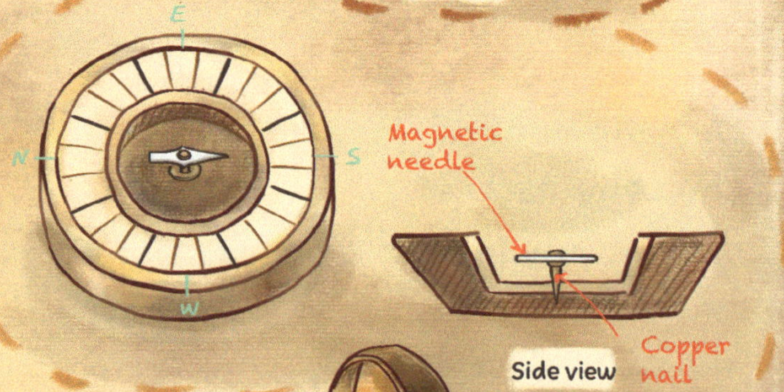

(4) Compass:

A non-floating compass with a combination of Chinese and Western styles

7

Challenge

When the pointer of the compass points to 18 degrees west of north, which Chinese character does it correspond to?

Hint: One circle equals 360 degrees; the angle formed by extending the calibration lines on either side of each Chinese character is 15 degrees.

Chapter 9

Going Home

Location: Earth   Weather: Clear

Yolk Pie seemed to sense a force on earth, easily directing the fleet in the right direction.

Soon, we returned to the island where our spaceship was located. We thanked the fleet commander and waved goodbye as they sailed away.

As they left, we heard the commander exclaim, "Huh? The compass is working properly again, ha-ha!"

With Yolk Pie, I found where the spaceship was parked. The ship was well hidden by the large banana leaves. The spaceship is intact. What a hidden good place!

Excitedly entering the ship, I asked Yolk Pie, "Since you have a location function, can you find your home?"

"Well, in theory, I can, but . . . I don't remember," replied Yolk Pie apologetically.

"Wait a minute, Yolk Pie, come over here. I just remembered something . . ."

Despite the struggle, I turned it over. "Ah? What's going on? Hey, what are you doing?"

"Ha-ha, just as I thought!" It turns out that Yolk Pie has a serial number on its body and a faint set of numbers under its bottom: 30° 11' 16" N, 120° 11' 12" E.

"Is this the exact location of your home?" I said to myself. With the thought of giving it a try, I entered the string of numbers into the spaceship system. Surprisingly, the system displayed: "Earth coordinates successfully located!" The time on the spaceship system also automatically switched to earth time!

"Wow, that's amazing!" Filled with anticipation, I pressed the time travel button.

In the blink of an eye, the ship traveled to another place. The buildings here were unlike any I had seen before.

There was a blue and white tower that looked like a giant standing with a half-circle head and two round ears on either side. In the center of the tower's top was a large red ring that sparkled brightly.

"That's it! That's it! That's my home!" shouted Yolk Pie, pointing to the tower. "Little fox, I'll take you to my home and introduce you to my magical friends!"

Although I was excited to meet Yolk Pie's magical friends, our time together was brief. Before we left, Yolk Pie gave me a device like a walkie-talkie so we could stay in touch.

Waving goodbye, I entered the spaceship and pressed the time travel button to return to the Math Planet.

Although reluctant, I eventually pressed the button to return to Math Planet . . .

In an instant, I was back on Math Planet.

I pushed open the door of my home, greeted my parents with feigned nonchalance, and then returned to my bedroom. Life on Math Planet was as calm as ever as if everything I had experienced was just a dream and nothing had happened.

I sat at my desk but was poked by something hard in my backpack. Suddenly, I remembered the walkie-talkie that Yolk Pie had given me before we parted ways. I quickly took it out of my backpack—

"Hello? Yolk Pie? Are you there?"

However, there was only a "zzz" noise from the walkie-talkie, and there was no response.

"Could it be because the distance is too far, and the signal can't be received? Alas . . ."

I sighed deeply and turned off the walkie-talkie in my hand. Scenes of adventures with Yolk Pie kept popping up, and my vision suddenly blurred. It seemed like something was flowing out of my eyes; my tears were falling with a pitter-patter sound.

"Yolk Pie . . . will it miss me?"

Knowledge Secret

How to locate the position on earth?

The longitude and latitude coordinate system allows you to determine any position on earth.

Latitude:

One circle of the equator is the 0° latitude line. North of the equator is the northern latitude; south of the equator is the southern latitude.

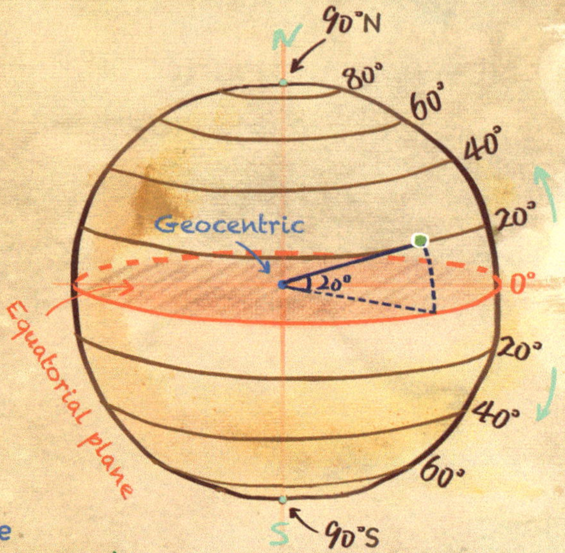

Latitude of a point: The line angle between the line connecting the point to earth's center and earth's equatorial plane.

Longitude of a point: The angle between the plane of longitude where the point is located and the plane where the 0° meridian is located.

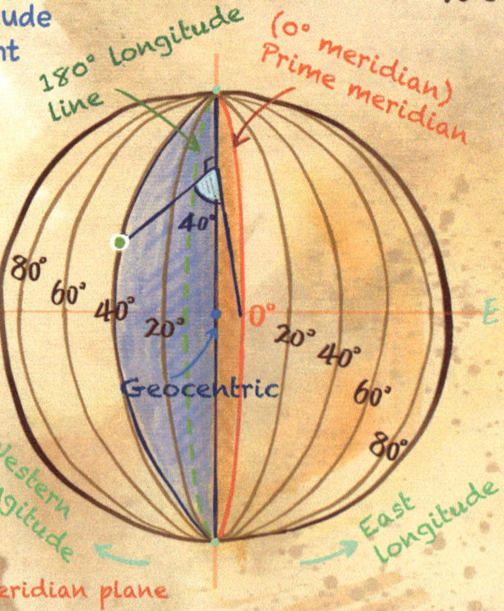

Longitude:

The prime meridian is 0° longitude. The eastward is east longitude, westward is west longitude. The east-west longitude coincides with 180° longitude.

The longitude and latitude divide earth into 360 and 180 parts in the vertical and horizontal directions respectively. However, the span between every two longitudes or every two latitudes is still very large. Therefore, below "degrees," it is possible to be precise down to "minutes" and "seconds."

60 seconds is 1 minute; 60 minutes is 1 degree.

Ancient Babylonian Hexadecimal

60" = 1

60' = 1

Which city corresponds to 120°E and 30°N?

Please find its corresponding city in the map below according to the geographical coordinates in the question.

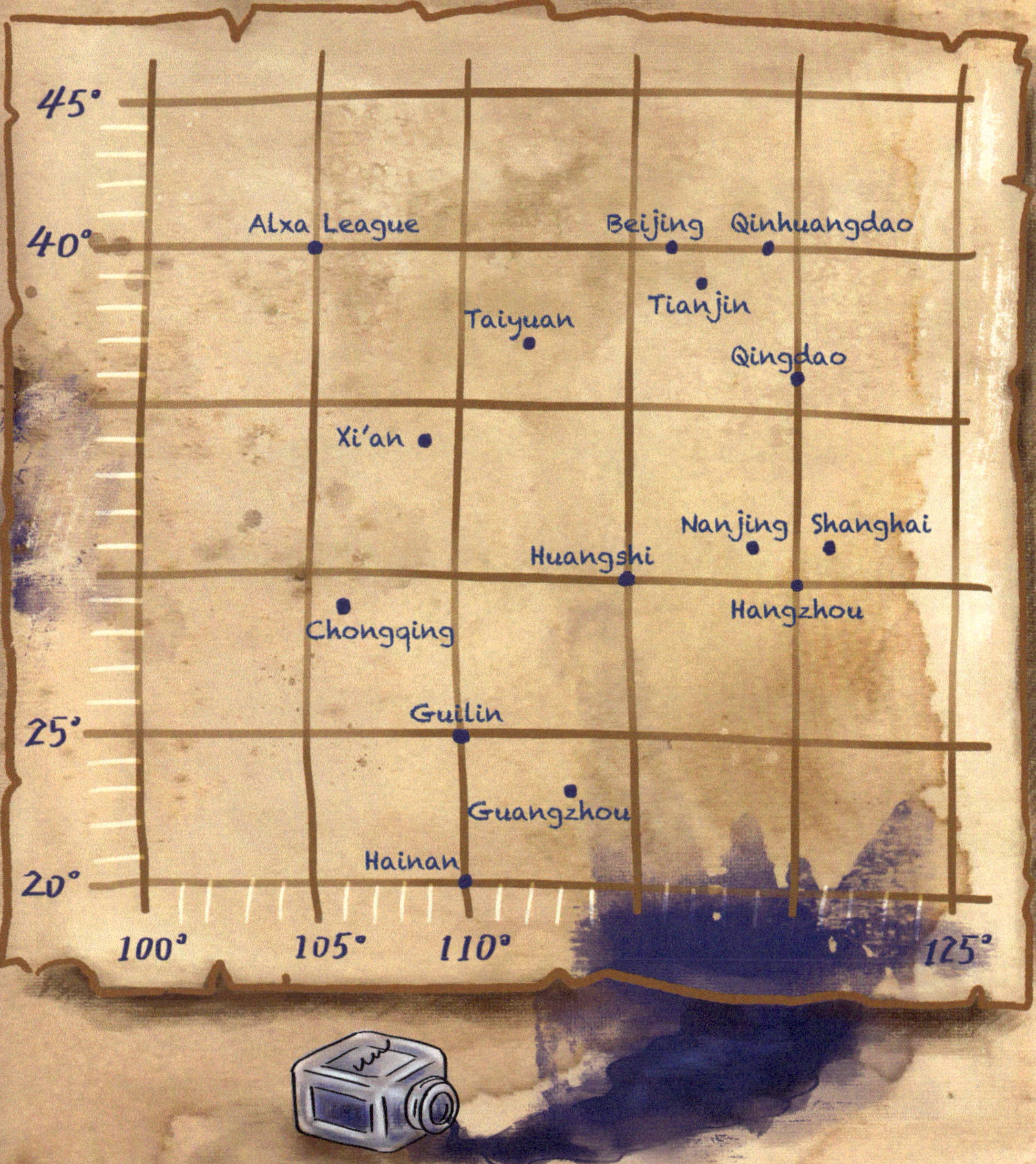

Decryption

Can you solve the challenge questions in each chapter?

Challenge 1	1 hour and 15 minutes
Challenge 2	E
Challenge 3	7
Challenge 4	Dog
Challenge 5	2:00 p.m.
Challenge 6	9
Challenge 7	Ren
Challenge 8	Hangzhou